Who Sat You Down?

Dr. Marlene Miles

Freshwater Press 2025

freshwaterpress9@gmail.com

ISBN: 978-1-967860-03-6

Paperback Version

Table of Contents

Who Sat You Down?

Freshwater

My Soul's So Happy

Sit down servant

I can't sit down

My soul's so happy

That I can't sit down

(Negro Spiritual)

When the zeal of the Lord is like fire shut up in your bones, how can you sit down? When the zeal for the House of God and the things of God consume you, how can you sit down?

for zeal for your house consumes me,
and the insults of those who insult you
fall on me. (Psalm 69:9)

Sometimes, even the people of God are made to sit down. Sometimes it is warranted and justified. Sometimes it is not. If you've ever been *sat down*, who did it? Was it God? Was it spoken through a mouthpiece of God? Was it you because you decided to stop like a stubborn mule? Was it your spouse or family with their soulish prayers and selfish requests because they wanted you to do something else? Or did you just get depressed?

Was it the enemy of our souls? Did he trick you? Did he trap you? Did he derail you and take you off course? Did he take you captive?

I pray that the things that matter to God will always matter to you and that you will do the will of Him who sent you. In so doing, your soul will be so happy that you must run on and pursue destiny, in the Name of Jesus, Amen.

God Told You Something

God told you something, then a man, a human, a person said something different; what do you do in that situation? How do you handle that?

There was a young prophet whom God sent to Bethel. God gave specific instructions, and the prophet went on his journey and did exactly what God said. After doing as he was told, leaving Bethel, on his way out of town he stopped to rest. That is when an older, seasoned prophet caught up with him and spoke lying words to him.

And went after the man of God, and found him sitting under an oak: and he said unto him, Art thou the man of God

that camest from Judah? And he said, I
am.

Then he said unto him, Come home with
me, and eat bread.

And he said, I may not return with thee,
nor go in with thee: neither will I eat
bread nor drink water with thee in this
place:

For it was said to me by the word of
the Lord, Thou shalt eat no bread nor
drink water there, nor turn again to go
by the way that thou camest.

He said unto him, I am a prophet also as
thou art; and an angel spake unto me by
the word of the Lord, saying, Bring him
back with thee into thine house, that he
may eat bread and drink water. But he
lied unto him.

So he went back with him, and did eat
bread in his house, and drank water.

And it came to pass, as they sat at the
table, that the word of the Lord came
unto the prophet that brought him back:

And he cried unto the man of God that came from Judah, saying, Thus saith the Lord, Forasmuch as thou hast disobeyed the mouth of the Lord, and hast not kept the commandment which the Lord thy God commanded thee,

But camest back, and hast eaten bread and drunk water in the place, of the which the Lord did say to thee, Eat no bread, and drink no water; thy carcase shall not come unto the sepulchre of thy fathers.

And it came to pass, after he had eaten bread, and after he had drunk, that he saddled for him the ~~ass~~, to wit, for the prophet whom he had brought back.

And when he was gone, a lion met him by the way, and slew him:
(1 Kings 13:14-24a)

Has God ever told you to do something then a man said, *Don't*, or a man said, *Not now*, or *Not yet*? Maybe a human said, *Not like that, but let's do it this way*. That can work in the opposite way too, a man wants something, but God says, No. Do you then persist to do it the way that the man wants? Or do you about face and do it God's way?

Balak wanted Balaam to curse Jacob. God said, No. Balak kept insisting, and that's how Balaam got stuck between a rock and a hard place on a donkey that turned and spoke to him, (Numbers 23).

God gave you the gift of tongues, but someone told you tongues is not real, but it is. So, do you continue praying in tongues, or do you quench the Holy Spirit, and not build up your faith by praying in your heavenly language?

God gave you a spiritual gift that is activated, but someone told you we don't do that here. I've been in churches that don't believe in prophecy. Do you also begin to ignore prophecy, or if you flow in that grace, that gift, or that office, do you continue there? Or, do you go to a location where your gift is acknowledged and used?

God said–, and you know you heard well, but then a man or woman shut you down. Do you abide by that? And if you do, for how long?

If God said it and gave directives and you didn't obey God--, why didn't you do it? Disobedience? Rebellion? Procrastination? Complete disobedience is the worst. But if you eventually obey God, that is still procrastination and that can cause great losses in your life and cause damage to your future and destiny. Are procrastinators testing or relying on the great patience of God and His being slow to anger?

By procrastination, rebellion or straight up disobedience you don't do what God says, what do you lose? How do you lose? **What do you lose when you lose a *spiritual* day?**

If God said a thing and then a man said something different, but you obeyed the human being, then who sinned?

Could the young prophet who was sent to Bethel say to God, if he were alive, "The old prophet told me?" Would that get him off the hook with God?

No, it would not.

Sometimes the devil will come along and say something else; sometimes it is not a human at all. After you disobey God, even though he incited it, that devil will then accuse you to God to make sure you get into trouble.

A Human Said Something Different

God said it. God told Adam he could eat from any tree in the Garden of Eden, but not the Tree of the Knowledge of Good and Evil. That's what God said, but then the devil said something else to Eve. It had partial truth in it, but just a little lie will pepper the thing and make it entirely too hot.

The Serpent told Eve something other than what God said, as if Eve had no ears. Of course, we don't know if Eve was present when God was talking to Adam. Most Bible scholars say that she was not there, and that the Serpent came to her separately from Adam and twisted God's words. After that, Eve transmitted the devil-distorted words to Adam. So, God said something to Adam and then a human, Eve, said something different to Adam.

Even then, Adam did that something else, something other than what God said.

Who sinned? Adam **and** Eve, they both sinned--, Eve, and her plus-one. Who was punished for the sins of Adam and Eve? **Both** were punished by curses, as well the lying Serpent was cursed.

God said something to Jonah. God told Jonah where he was to go and what he was to do there. God told Jonah to go to Ninevah and preach repentance to the people there. Jonah didn't like the Ninevites, so he decided to go in the opposite direction of Ninevah. That's not what God said, though.

We've made mention now of God saying something or giving a directive, but then a *lying spirit,* the Serpent came and changed what God said, in essence stopping humans from doing what God said.

Now we've moved into rebellion and disobedience where the person that God gave a directive to decides on their own, possibly with spiritual influence--, it is not stated in the Bible. But, the person of their own accord decides to do something different than what God said.

Who told Jonah to do something different? Jonah did.

God told David in the Word and in the Law not to do something, but with Bathsheba, David did something different. Everyone who knows the Word and does the opposite is guilty of sin.

God told David what to do regarding the taking of the census, but David disobeyed God and did something different. Again, the person that told David something different than what God had said was David. It was the person himself.

God said certain things to Solomon, but Solomon did something other than what God said. God told Solomon not to marry those strange women. They were called strange because they served other *gods*. They did not serve Jehovah God, but they were from all over and worshipped many different idol *gods*. The Lord God didn't just tell Solomon not to marry them as most parents might say, **Because I said so**. God even told Solomon <u>*why*</u> which is something every human three years old and up wants to know--, *why* he was not to marry those women; but Solomon disobeyed.

Marrying them in the Bible meant having sex with them--, even once. If they had sex, in the Bible, they were married. **<u>It still means that.</u>** Now, Solomon probably thought, with all of his Wisdom, that he got from God, that he wouldn't burn incense and give sacrifices, and whatever else these women were doing that constituted worship, so Solomon probably figured that he'd be okay. He probably figured that he's not really worshipping if he doesn't go to their temple, shrine, or altar. But that's not true.

Solomon is one of the subjects in my book, **By Means of a Whorish Father:** *What Happens to the Children?* because whether in the natural Solomon worshipped those idol *gods*, by virtue of sleeping with those women–, even once, Solomon would be worshiping what they worshipped. Saints of God, it is deeper than that. People that you have friendships and alliances with, people you spend time with-, there can be a transference of spirits, unless the Holy Spirit in you is enlarged and empowered enough to withstand the transfer.

Another disobedient human. We must not think we are wiser than God. After all, if we have Wisdom, we got it from God. So how are we now smarter than our Teacher?

Further, we must not think that it is only what we see that actually happens in life.

Who Sat You Down?

God said something; He gave a directive. You didn't do it; you don't even talk about it anymore. Who shut you up? Did you let shyness or insecurity shut you up? Did you let a jealous human make you stop saying what God told you to say? Or, did you just decide, that's not cool, so I'm not doing it?

Who shut you down? Did you lose heart? Did depression make you give up? Or did a man, a woman, another human in some authority over you shut you down?

Yes, there are levels of respect that we must honor in life. God is a God of order. He has a hierarchy of authority. We should respect that spiritual authority, as well as natural authority.

The Word says that we are not to be respecters of persons, that means treating the rich and affluent better than we treat the poor. But, people do it. We have to be told because it is human nature to do that.

Ye shall not **respect** persons in judgment; *but* ye shall hear the small as well as the great; ye shall not be afraid of the face of man; for the judgment *is* God's: and the cause that is too hard for you, bring *it* unto me, and I will hear it. (Deuteronomy 1:17)

For there is no **respect** of persons with God.The rich and the poor, God made them both. (Romans 2:11)

Thou shalt not wrest judgment; thou shalt not **respect** persons, neither take a gift: for a gift doth blind the eyes of the wise, and pervert the words of the righteous. (Deuteronomy 16:19)

Sometimes a person is "shut down" or stays sat down because they never get an opportunity to stand up. A poor man's wisdom is seldom heard. Sometimes affluent people are allowed to speak or be used even in ministry while the anointed person may be still parked on the pew. God said to you, but money said to the person who decides who is going to run the Bible Study.

This is not always the case, and we pray that it is never the case, but often it is. I was a member of a church where if you were a tither or a strong giver then you automatically had a leadership position in that church. That doesn't make sense because the strong givers have higher paying jobs usually. That doesn't make them more anointed, necessarily.

If you are in a "church" where people are buying positions, it might do you well to get out of there, unless God sent you for a specific reason.

Wherefore now let the fear of the LORD be upon you; take heed and do *it*: for *there is* no iniquity with the LORD our God, nor **respect** of

persons, nor taking of gifts.
(2 Chronicles 19:7)

To have **respect** of persons *is* not
good: for for a piece of
bread *that* man will transgress.
(Proverbs 28:21)

Not one of us can buy our way
into Heaven.

Honour thy father and thy mother: that
thy days may be long upon the
land which the LORD thy
God giveth thee. (Exodus 20:12)

A young woman wanted to be a
dentist. Her father was a dentist, but he
told her that women are not dentists.

In the year he died, that woman
enrolled in dental school. She did not
disrespect her father by going to dental
school when he told her not to. Instead,
she became a dental hygienist and
honored her father. But in the year that he
died, she began to do what was really in
her heart to do. Whether God gave her that
dream or whether it was her own dream;
she did not disrespect her father.

In the year that king Uzziah died I saw also the Lord sitting upon a throne, high and lifted up, and his train filled the temple. (Isaiah 6:1)

Isaiah was already a prophet, why had he not seen God? Was Uzziah blocking something, or blocking Isaiah in some way? Sometimes the voice that is disrupting your life has to be quiet so you can do what God said to do. For the woman who wanted to go to dental school, in the year that her father died, I saw her in dental school I know because I was there, and she was my friend. Was her father blocking her?

There are blockers in this world. You need courage and boldness to do what you're supposed to do, even if people laugh at you or mock you. Did Noah build an ark?

Yes.

Was Noah mocked?

Yes.

Don't let people purposefully or inadvertently shut you down by mocking, or undermining your confidence.

Know what you believe and know how to defend it. Know how to speak what you believe and believe in. Unbelievers and sinners surely know what they believe in. They could be completely wrong, but they are usually completely confident and will gladly spout off what they know, or what they've figured out.

The, it *don't* take all that crowd is a naysaying, blocker crowd. They may be full of disbelief, mischief, or both.

Maybe it does take all that. If you have ever seen or ever been that person who is massively oppressed or even possessed by the devil, it does take all that. Not all that in the flesh, but spiritually it takes all that. Six thousand demons came out of Legion. That didn't look hard to Jesus according to the Bible account, but that was Jesus. **Jesus is all that**, therefore it took **all that**. When the

Disciples couldn't cast an evil *spirit* out of a little boy Jesus told them that some only come out by prayer and fasting. So, in the Gadarenes do you think the Disciples could have cast 6000 devils out of Legion?

See, it took **all that**. It took Jesus.

There are some who lost everything for their disobedience and disrespect of authority and or anointing. One example is King Saul. Of course, he thought he was the ultimate authority. Perhaps in the physical, he was, but God is the highest spiritual authority and is therefore God over all.

Remember those who rule over you, who have spoken the word of God to you, whose faith follow, considering the outcome of *their* conduct.

Do not be carried about with various and strange doctrines. For *it is* good that the heart be established by grace, not with foods which have not profited those who have been occupied with them. (Hebrews 13:7-9)

Have respect for those who have rule over you and as David did, never disrespect the anointing of another.

Therefore, when God gives a directive, a command, He also provides empowerment or anointing for that thing. So, if God told you to do something and a human stopped you, they came up against the anointing of God. God's Word will not return to Him void, so what happens to the anointing on a Word that God wants fulfilled but the person assigned that Word is not working it? God doesn't waste. He doesn't pour anointing out on the ground; it accomplishes what He sends it to do.

The person who stopped you, interfered with you, interfered with the anointing and with the plans of God. God's plans are not loosey goosey and haphazard. God is not on island time, and no one is chugging beers or sipping margaritas. God is a man of business and is conducting business in the Earth and we all work for Him. Well, we either work for

Him or against Him; it is a binary decision.

Some lost everything, some were not turned over to death, but they suffered affliction for not obeying God. Jonah is a good example of that.

Did You Sit Yourself Down?

A person could just say, I'm taking a break, or a hiatus and stop doing what they were formerly doing. If God approved that, then that should turn into a very nice prayer retreat or sabbatical. But if you sat down just because you felt like taking a break, or you were tired of "not having any fun," you are at risk of losing at least a lot, and at most, everything.

If you "sat down" so you could feel like you're "*normal*" bowing to poor pressure so you could do what your friends are doing for a while, that is so unwise. God can fix burn-out and restore your joy; just ask Him. Going out into the world to be worldly is not going to build up your energy reserves. It will be even more draining. Sitting down just because you don't feel you're effective or you are not appreciated is not wise either.

Worse than that, you could be sat down by the enemy, which would be one of his daily goals anyway. In pursuit of worldly pleasures, when a person sins, there is iniquity and that is also how souls are captured by the enemy. Once captured, a person is in captivity. Captivity is the same as being **sat down**, not just because you are, but it may mean that your anointing doesn't work anymore, or that it doesn't work like it used to, through you.

And Jesus said unto him, No man, having put his hand to the plough, and looking back, is fit for the kingdom of God. (Luke 9:62)

You may have seen people who were seriously anointed, but now they chase sin, and it shows. They are flat and ineffective. They've grieved and quenched the Holy Spirit and He may have just stopped talking to them.

The fact that David prayed that the Lord not take His Spirit from him indicates that that is possible.

> Cast me not away from thy presence;
> and take not thy holy spirit from me.
> (Psalm 51:11)

Yet, we read that the gifts of God are without repentance, which means God doesn't remove a spiritual gift from you that He has given you? Well, the gifts work by Love. God is Love, and if you are not in relationship with God, then what power will you use to "work" the gift that you still have?

Even if you fit into one or more of these categories, don't lose hope because as long as there is life, there is hope. Repent and ask God to restore you to right relationship and to restore the Holy Spirit so you are spiritually alive and not spiritually dead.

Did God Sit You Down?

If it wasn't your own decision, to disobey God, did the person who sat you down speak as a mouthpiece of the Lord? Or, did they speak out of their own jealousy, anger, or other nefarious agenda?

When someone does something wrong you go to them in private. If they don't heed, then you go with a witness as in an intervention. If that doesn't work, then you may take it public. But if no one has spoken to you about an actual error or fault, then where is your spiritual due process? If there is no due process that's rather an indication that this is not of God, at least it is not being handled God's way.

God sat people down in the Bible, of course He calls it rejecting them. Saul was rejected for his rebellion. God gave Saul a whole lot of chances though, didn't He?

So, the Lord rejected the descendants of Israel in His divine judgment against the Northern Kingdom that was rife with idolatry and disobedience to God's covenant. That rejection was because of the Israelites consistently breaking their covenant with God.

Being rejected by God is a terrible thing; it is spiritual death. Rejected by God means He rejects your position, your authority, your priesthood. That means that your sacrifices, offerings, and even prayers are not being heard or answered. These rejections may be when prayers become sin, and God is not listening. They could be caused by having an ought (issue) with your brother.

Rejection of Saul was evident when Saul didn't wait for Samuel and tried to be priest and do offerings, and that was not his place.

Nadab and Abihu offered up strange fire before the Lord, and that was an abomination. Phineas and Hophni, Eli's sons kept the best portions of the offerings for themselves. As well these two who served as priests, were sleeping with the temple prostitutes so their priesthood was unclean and rejected.

And Nadab and Abihu, the sons of Aaron, took either of them his censer, and put fire therein, and put incense thereon, and offered strange fire before the Lord, which he commanded them not. And there went out fire from the Lord, and devoured them, and they died before the Lord. (Leviticus 10:1-3)

Annais and Sapphira were rejected because of their fake offerings, and they dropped dead.

Who Put You Outside the Gates?

For disobedience, some were turned over to affliction, but not to death. That is the Mercy of God. But, how much time, how much momentum, how much progress has any person lost for not doing what God said, when God said it, and even how God said? Then there are some who have lost time, momentum, progress, and blessings. For example, the watchman on the wall must declare what God tells him to tell others, else the blood of any who are lost is on the hands of that watchman.

Disobedience to God is not really a choice if you want to live and have a blessed life. And, in that wise, you cannot let people advise you over what God has told you. You cannot let people turn you from what God has told you. You cannot let even a seasoned prophet who is a liar lead you another way contrary to what the Lord has told you.

You also cannot choose sin yourself, or let yourself be tricked into sin, rebellion or disobedience. Any sin blocks you from doing what God said. Any defilement can put you outside the gate.

What gate?

The gate to the city. The gate to the Kingdom. The gate into the Courts of the Lord. While you are outside the gate, how much spiritual progress did you lose that day that you were outside of the gate?

Any sin or defilement puts you outside the gate for at least a day. How much spiritual progress do you lose in a day?

We enter into His gates with Thanksgiving. The ascension is next you enter into the Courts of the Lord with Praise. If you can't get into the gates, how are you going to get to the Courts? Outside the gates means that your thanksgiving is not working, it is not heard. We are silenced ourselves if we are outside of the range of God. Our endeavor is to not sin and to not be defiled. Therefore, we must be undefileable. How is that possible?

And you can't enter into the holy of holies, which is worship because you are **outside** the gate for sinning or having been defiled.

So we are never outside the gate, or at least in Thanksgiving. If we are outside of the gate that means we can't get to the Courts of the Lord. We can't get into praise that day--, the whole day. God inhabits the praises of His people. How or why would God come to you if you are not praising Him? The final ascension is into worship--, the Holy of Holies. But how will you get there if not through the Gates and the Courts of the Lord?

Jealous of the Anointing

Saul was jealous of David. Basically, he was jealous of David's anointing. Herod was jealous of Jesus' star; basically, he was jealous of Jesus' anointing.

Pharisees and Sanhedrin Council were jealous of Jesus. Jealousy is the root of so much evil. It was the impetus for the first murder in the Bible.

A person has got to be one of the craziest people ever to be jealous of another person's anointing. Of course, jealousy is a work of the flesh, and it is a spirit, so a person may be oppressed or possessed by that spirit and therefore crazy with jealousy. We all need deliverance somewhere, so seek deliverance. God is Father to us all, and as our parent, He loves all His children, so there is no need for jealousy. Everything that is for you is for you. Endeavor to meet the conditions to receive the blessings that God has for you. How do you think you can meet the conditions to receive the blessings that God has for your sibling, or your neighbor, or a celebrity? Your obedience, your blessings are what you should focus on.

If you are chosen to by God to fly across the country on a certain assignment, God will give you the Grace, the anointing, even the provision to do that. Let's say that provision is $1000. There may be another person who is given $500 to fly halfway across the country to do something that will be only ½ as difficult. For both assignments, God gives the provision, anointing and Grace. Doesn't the person who has more to do need more anointing? Might they need more Grace? God knows. Might they need more provision? Yes.

So, how can any of us be jealous of what God has told another person to do and how much it's going to **cost** that person spiritually, physically, emotionally? Sleepless nights? Fastings? Prayer watches? Sacrifices and offerings? Nurturing their relationship with God and walking in consecration and holiness?

You cannot think that because you have to go ½ the way across the country, you should get your own 500 dollars **and** the other person's 1000 so they go nowhere, and you have extra anointing that has nothing to do with you? Are you sane, right now?

Jesus was born in Bethlehem and He had an incredible star. It was seen in the East and even Wise Men came to worship Him. Jesus' assignment on Earth was not only massive, but it was also difficult, it was critical and important, dangerous, perilous.

Herod is jealous of Jesus. It started out with the Star of Bethlehem, as we will call it. Why would Herod need a star like that? To do what with it? Live a life of luxury, be carnal, and be evil to people?

Of course, we know it is for the power, the money and the fame because no matter what God intended the anointing to be used for, the one who wants to steal anointing is planning to misuse it. Being jealous of another's calling, Grace, star, purpose or destiny says that you didn't think that God did it right, or that God doesn't know what He is doing. But God certainly knows what He is doing.

Folks, none of us need anointing to be carnal. Being fleshy, in the flesh and of the flesh does not require anointing. That comes naturally with the sin nature that we are born into.

Divine Appointments

You can't just let any old thing happen to you spiritually. You have to stay praised up, prayed up, and paid up, as in sacrifices. If you are outside of the Gate, then you are outside of fellowship with the Lord. And you are outside of fellowship with God's people, for a whole day, at least.

The next morning, we get tender mercies. Surely, we don't sin as soon as we wake up, negating the tender mercies that the Lord just gave us. But, then again, it depends on where you wake up. If you wake up in the sin you fell asleep in, there is a real possibility that sin is waiting to defile you right then. If you are still there in your sin, in your polluted blood, your intention may very well be to keep sinning.

Stay prayed up. Praised up. Walk upright before the Lord. Because if you are outside the Gate, you are outside of fellowship and communion with the Lord. For a whole day if tender mercies don't start again until the next morning.

Does that divine appointment come around again? If so, when? Do you think it keeps repeating day after day until you get it right, as in a movie? Sometimes the Holy Spirit will give us heads up on where to go when and that we may meet such and such a person there. But sometimes even divine appointments are pure serendipity.

Does that divine connection come back again? If so, when? How will you know if it will or not? Divine appointments are on divine destiny clocks. When people sin, they get off the correct timing for their lives. Therefore, we must all try to stay on our divine clock. If necessary, we must get our destiny clock reset, unbroken, or put back together. This all depends on what happened to our destiny clock in the first place. The devil likes to sabotage destiny clocks and does all kinds of things to those clocks. If a person's timing is off, their entire life may reflect that.

Signs that you are off your destiny clock, the clock that God has established for your life include, relationship and business failures, money losses, always going *through* or in tough times, making no progress, can't get ahead. Conmen find you; you are easily conned. You are at the wrong church or have a satanic pastor. You want to be married, but where is your spouse? A person is educated, but they have no job. You have a job, but there are no advancements. This puts you into evil timelines and ropes a person into a counterfeit life.

(From the message, *Recovery of Your Divine Destiny Clock,*

https://www.youtube.com/watch?v=JNGVG8 GyvUM). Stay to the end and do the prayers to get your destiny clock back and reset to God's timing for your life.

Get your Star back. Keep yourself walking upright. Stay in fellowship with God and with God's people. Sometimes defilement is about taking your virtues, your blessings, your glory--, your star.

(*Star Bright* – Powerful prayer on Dr. Marlene Miles You Tube channel: https://www.youtube.com/watch?v=POiop-HIa14)

Even in the natural, when you miss a bus, a train, a plane, or the cruise you were supposed to be on for your vacation, aren't you pretty upset? Then should you not be more upset if you miss an opportunity that God has for you? We should not take these things for granted that everything we miss because of sitting down, or being sat down is an opportunity that will come back around again.

A human or some evil entity changed your mind, or your thought process so you disobeyed God. This human or spiritual entity may have caused you to be *defiled* so you wouldn't receive the blessings that God had for you that day, that season, or in that time period.

If you miss your vehicle of destiny, how will you get to the next place in God?

Your vehicle of destiny must be properly used and maintained. If you miss the vehicle that is supposed to take you there or to your next destination, how will you get there, and when?

Get back into your correct timeline. That's where your divine connections and appointments are, whether you know about them or whether they are a complete and Godly surprise for you. Sin will jump you out of your Godly timeline because while what God has planned for your life is moving forward as a vehicle that you should be on, you are parked outside the gate for a whole day or longer. It depends on how long you persist in sin. It depends on if you have repented and renounced that sin or not. It depends on whether you sat down or gave up instead of moving forward. It depends on if you think you are being obedient by obeying a human while disobeying God and are simply stationary and sitting down. It depends on how long you are defiled, get defiled and do nothing about it.

Folks, defilement is horrible, but if you try to do something about it, God will help you. But if you give up or do nothing, then God will think you just agree with it. Again, *defiled* means outside the Gate for a day.

What do you lose when you lose a spiritual day? Or week? Or a month? A year? A decade?

The Wilderness Timeline

Does this ring a bell? 40 years trying to get somewhere that should have taken 11 days, and they never got in – their kids did, but they did not even get in. I speak of the Israelites in the Wilderness trying to get to and into the Promised Land.

What were the delays? To name a few: idolatry, soul ties with sin. Missing the garlic and leeks, and cucumbers. Murmuring, complaining. God is providing free food--, manna, but they wanted meat.

So, the Wilderness answer is any delay, every delay can be devastating, treacherous or even deadly. These people didn't miss one hour or one day. They didn't miss one bus, train, plane or one cruise ship. Now you can see that individuals can have a destiny clock, as well as a collective of people can be on or off their destiny clock. The Israelites in the Wilderness missed 40 years. In those days, that was a lifetime. And it surely was a lifetime because they were stuck outside the gate, and they died outside the gate. That gate was the *Gate* to the Promised Land.

Yes, it had a gate, and that gate repelled them. It could also have been that they repulsed the Gate. With a gate, often you need a key or a code. The code to get in through the Gate to the Promised Land was covenant with God and God had made covenant with these folks, but they weren't upholding their end. So, when they got to (or near) the Gate, the gatekeeper could say, "Show me your credentials." If they had no credentials, then the person they were with could say, "They are with Me."

They were supposed to have been able to say that because they were supposed to have been with God. Instead, they were with sinners and idols and idol *gods*. Therefore, they couldn't unlock or override the **lock** on the Gate and were kept out instead of being allowed in.

There are invisible, spiritual gates in front of a whole lot of things and blessings that God has for you. The enemy erects these gates, but if you are not in God--, all the way in, things you do or don't do could block you. In this case: sin and iniquity kept them outside of the Gate to the Promised Land.

40 years.

Sin takes people out of their correct and Godly timelines. This is linear but consider this: There are 33 11-day cycles in a year. That means if you count off 11 days, in a month you will get approximately 3 of them. In a year there will be 33 11-day cycles. In the Wilderness, even if the Israelites messed up on the first 11 days of getting to the Promised Land, there were approximately two more 11-day cycles in that same month to get from Egypt to Canaan. In a year there were 33 11-day cycles. Thirty-three times they could have gotten to the Promised Land in a year.

In 40 years, let's do the math: there were 1327 11-day cycles in 40 years, where the Israelites could have made it to the land that God had promised them. That's in the very least. They may not have had to wait a whole eleven days to start the cycle again each time, which means they had **more** than 33 times to make it in in a year. Well, they had 365 different days in a year they could have made it into the Promised Land. If you are still counting 11-day cycles, they had at least 1327 times to make it in in 40 years. Actually, there are 14,600 days in 40 years. Yet, they never made it in.

Their children made it in, but they did not.

Don't you give your kids things to do that you know they can do, things you know they can accomplish? And don't you help them to do it? **With God**, ALL things are possible. God would not have gotten the Hebrews out of Egypt and sent them on an impossible journey; they should have made it into the Promised Land.

Not succeeding in 40 years at something that should have taken 11 days speaks of all the things we've been talking about in this book. Distraction, yes. Broken destiny clock? Yes. But it is as though that Wilderness crowd of Israelites either rebelliously sat themselves down like stubborn mules, or they went into sin, bondage, and captivity and let the devil sit them down. At one point they let an evil report--, hold them back. God didn't say they couldn't get in, but a man said something different.

And Caleb stilled the people before Moses, and said, Let us go up at once, and possess it; for we are well able to overcome it.

But the men that went up with him said, We be not able to go up against the people; for they are stronger than we.

And they brought up an evil report of the land which they had searched unto the children of Israel, saying, The land, through which we have gone to search it, is a land that eateth up the inhabitants thereof; and all the people that we saw in it are men of a great stature (Numbers 13:30-33)

They lost 40 years; they lost their lives *outside* the Gate. They were outside that Gate long enough to die.

Every delay could be devastating, treacherous, or even deadly. So you never want to get off God's divine timing for your life by sin, defilement, or by the false words of any person with authority over you. But the dilemma is that you still must respect authority.

What Did You Miss?

God works outside of time, but flesh doesn't. When you miss a day, you could miss a divine connection, a divine appointment, or a divine opportunity. Will it come back around for you? Only God knows.

So, pray and ask Him.

If you are going somewhere, but you miss your arrival by 11 days, that can be a great concern depending on what you were to do with the connection and the destination. But saints of God, when you miss your target by 40 years, that's an entire generation. In the land where God has promised you, all kinds of weeds and wild animals could have grown up in it and taken it over. A full generation or two of human squatters could have taken over the land, so now when you get there to go in, you can't because the obstacles have had a chance to entrench themselves there and wax bold.

Simply put, if you wash the lasagna pan tonight after dinner it is so much easier to clean than if you wait until morning when everything is crusty and stuck on the dish or pan. Time matters. If you take the weeds out of your flower garden weekly, it will be so much easier than if you do it monthly. So, if you do what God says to do, when God says, you could save yourself a world of trouble and also ensure your own success.

The Israelites had to fight the Hittites, the Girgashites, the Amorites, the Canaanites, the Perizzites, the Hivites, and the Jebusites. There were more tribes in the Bible, but those are the main seven. Seven is a number of perfection, so there were many enemies to deal with.

I challenge that had they gotten to the Promised Land in the eleven days, those opposing nations either would not have been there or in the area, or on the way. Or they may not have been there in strength and number and magnitude.

Time matters.

When you get *there* matters as much as *if* you get there. Wherever, **there** is.

If you're to take a prayer watch, for example, but you don't, what do you miss because you were tired and wanted to sleep more? God said. Who countered what God said? Was it you? Was it laziness? Was it a sleep wave? That is an enemy attack; if you were planning spiritual warfare that is the enemy attacking you before you can attack him.

Who disobeyed God? Who talked back to God?

What did you miss by not taking the watch? Will you ever know? If you are the one who turned back over and went back to sleep instead of getting up for the prayer watch there is no witch, devil or demon you can blame. You did it.

Who talked back to God when God was talking? What if a visitation from the Lord was to happen during or after this prayer session? Did you miss God? Who were you supposed to be praying for? What condition are they in now because you didn't pray for them? What did you miss, and who missed you? What might the person you should have been interceding for miss?

God said, "Raise an altar." Did you? What or who stopped you? Do you think God just told you to do that just for fun? If God is talking, there is a reason for it. Just as when you are speaking to your own children, there is a reason that you are talking to them, telling them something, or imparting knowledge or Wisdom to them.

So, whether you obeyed God and raised that altar or not, that's between you and God, but realize that sowing is for your future. I don't know of any seeds that come up the day after you plant them. I don't know of any seeds that harvest at the same hour they are planted. Still, God works outside of Time; He can do as He pleases.

What did you miss by not raising an altar if God said do it? You may not know until some future time when that seed should harvest, but you have nothing if you planted nothing or planted at the wrong time.

Nothing Requires Nothing

If you were born and raised in a house where your parents required nothing of you then you did not have a Godly model growing up. God gives us unconditional love, but covenant has conditions. In order to have covenant with God, there are conditions. God loves us unconditionally, but covenant has conditions.

Where in the Bible does God say I'm going to make covenant with you but nothing is required of you? No, there are conditions.

Your parents do not have a covenant with you. If you are overly connected to your parents those are either soul ties, apron strings, or both. Your parents have a covenant with each other, but not with their children. You have to be at the age of accountability or legally an adult to make agreements, contracts, and covenants in the natural.

You grow up and go out into the world and make your own covenants. That means that things between you two who are in covenant together are mutually agreed upon. You are not saved by your parents' covenant with God. You are not saved because your grandmother is saved or goes to church; you must establish our own relationship with God and make your own covenant with God as well.

God said, *That I may establish covenant with you,* so there are conditions. He said to Noah, **Be fruitful and multiply and take the animals with you.**

Go forth of the ark, thou, and thy wife, and thy sons, and thy sons' wives with thee. (Genesis 8:16)

Go with your wife, Noah. Your sons will go with their wives. This is part of the covenant. People are supposed to be married. It says so in the Bible, that's not just me talking.

Bring forth with thee every living thing that is with thee, of all flesh, both of fowl, and of cattle, and of every creeping thing that creepeth upon the earth; that they may breed abundantly in the earth, and be fruitful, and multiply upon the earth.
(Genesis 8:16-17)

Breeding abundantly is one of the conditions. God multiplying is one of the perks of this covenant.

With Abraham, God changed his name from Abram. God gave him land and God says He will be their God and keep covenant with them. Another part of the covenant is that God says they will be circumcised. That is part of the covenant-, circumcision. Not all religions have a covenant that requires circumcision, but for the Jew, wouldn't a man be reminded several times a day of his covenant relationship with God? And God might have chosen circumcision on that particular body part for many reasons. First God is making Abraham the **father** of many nations and he will have many descendants. Typical of God--, give me part of a thing that I will bless and multiply back to you. Further because of sexual sin being so common, this should be a reminder for a man, several times a day, so that he does not get into so much trouble with reproductive body parts.

Abrahamic covenant:

As for me, behold, my covenant *is* with thee, and thou shalt be a father of many nations. Neither shall thy name any more be called Abram, but thy name shall be Abraham; for a father of many nations have I made thee. And I will make thee exceeding fruitful, and I will make nations of thee, and kings shall come out of thee. And I will establish my covenant between me and thee and thy seed after thee in their generations for an everlasting covenant, to be a God unto thee, and to thy seed after thee.

And I will give unto thee, and to thy
seed after thee, the land wherein thou
art a stranger, all the land of Canaan,
for an everlasting possession; and I will
be their God.

And God said unto Abraham, Thou shalt
keep my covenant therefore, thou, and
thy seed after thee in their generations.

This *is* my covenant, which ye shall
keep, between me and you and thy seed
after thee; Every man child among you
shall be circumcised. (Genesis 17:7)

Then God established covenants
with Isaac, Jacob, and so forth. Covenant
is between at least two people, and it has
requirements; usually the lesser is blessed
by the greater.

God is greater.

Obedience is part of every
covenant with God.
So, when God says something; in order to
keep covenant you **do** that something.

Who Do You Obey?

Obey them that have the rule over you,
and submit yourselves: for they watch
for your souls, as they that must give
account, that they may do it with joy,
and not with grief: for that is
unprofitable for you. (Hebrews 13:17)

God said--, but here comes someone else and says something else. What are you going to do now? Would you rather obey man or God? Depends on who is speaking and what authority they have over you, right?

You can know whether to obey them or not by **trying** the *spirits*. Who said it? What *spirit* is motivating the person who said it? Who do you love more?

Joseph obeyed God and ended up in slavery and then prison, but he loved God more than himself and man.

Daniel obeyed God, was put in the fiery furnace, but God got him out safely. Daniel was also put in the lion's den ,but God brought him out of that, as well.

Jesus obeyed God, but after God had *said*, and Jesus is making the plans to obey, here comes the voice of Peter, who said something opposite to what God had already spoken. Peter said something that did not line up with what God had said.

Jesus prayed fervently in Gethsemane asking the Father if this *cup* could pass from Him, but He ended up doing the will of God. Jesus ended up on the Cross, but that was the plan of God. And, He asked God and not Peter and not any other human what He must do or could do. He spoke with the Person who had given Him the assignment or directive.

Then charged he his disciples that they should tell no man that he was Jesus the Christ. From that time forth began Jesus to shew unto his disciples, how that he must go unto Jerusalem, and suffer many things of the elders and chief priests and scribes, and be killed, and be raised again the third day.

Then Peter took him, and began to rebuke him, saying, Be it far from thee, Lord: this shall not be unto thee. But he turned, and said unto Peter, Get thee behind me, Satan: thou art an offence unto me: for thou savourest not the things that be of God, but those that be of men.

Then said Jesus unto his disciples, If any *man* will come after me, let him deny himself, and take up his cross, and follow me. For whosoever will save his life shall lose it: and whosoever will lose his life for my sake shall find it.

For what is a man profited, if he shall gain the whole world, and lose his own soul? or what shall a man give in exchange for his soul?
(Matthew 16:20-26)

What shall it profit you to please a man, a person, even a person in authority over you if it is not what God said? What profit is it to gain the world and lose your own soul? If a person's soul is at risk because of man-pleasing when it is not what God said to do, then why take that risk? If your soul is at risk because of disobeying God, then why take that risk? When you man-please, people-please, you may earn accolades for the time being, but what about your soul? What about your destiny? What about eternity? What about the progress you were making, spiritually? **STOP** the people-pleasing.

I will not be afraid, for what can man do to me? (Psalms 56:11)

In God have I put my trust: I will not be afraid what man can do unto me.

And,

The LORD *is* on my side; I will not fear: what can man do unto me?
(Psalms 118.6)

Test the Spirits

Try every *spirit*. Ask the Holy Spirit, "Who said that?" "What *spirit* is behind what I was just told?"

(A portion of this chapter is from the book, **the spirit of error: paving the way for Antichrist**.)

If you hear a word in your heart, in your spirit and your first response is, "Lord, is that You?" That's a better response if you are not absolutely sure than to just believe that *spirit or that voice*. Don't believe the *spirit* just because you heard it and it is a spiritual phenomenon; the devil is also a *spirit*, and his entities are also *spirits*.

Recall, the Lord called Samuel three times before he realized it was the Lord who was calling him and not Eli. The point is that you don't know whose voice is calling you. You don't know who is speaking to you—, until you know. Make sure you know and are not just guessing.

Beloved, do not believe every spirit, but test the spirits to see whether they are from God, because many false prophets have gone out into the world.
(1 John 4:1 NASB)

False prophets have always been out and about. Recall the story from the opening of this book from 1 Kings 13 where the young prophet was deceived by an older prophet while on an assignment from God. The devil roams about as a roaring lion looking for whom he may devour. In this case the young prophet was killed, but not devoured by the lion.

We must **discern** liars, *lying spirits*, false prophecy, lies-, false pastors, falsehoods. We discern *error*, so we can **LIVE!!!**

Jesus didn't have to *try* the *spirit* that was speaking through Peter, He knew who it was right away. For that reason, we know that Jesus knew that Satan had entered Judas as well.

Peter didn't know how wrong he was; he thought he was only showing "love" to Jesus. *I want the best for you* is the sentiment of most people in the natural. The best is God's best. The best is God's plan; but if we don't know what God's plan is for another then how can we agree on it? The only way is to say and pray that when you pray for someone with the understanding, *"May the will of God be done in your life."* Else, pray in the Spirit so the Holy Spirit can interpret what we are saying to the Lord. Amen.

Peter is the one who cut off the centurion's ear and Jesus healed it.

When Jesus' followers saw what was going to happen, they said, "Lord, should we strike with our swords?" [50] And one of them struck the servant of the high priest, cutting off his right ear.

But Jesus answered, "No more of this!" And he touched the man's ear and healed him. (Luke 22:49-51)

God's plan will go forth with or without you. Further, you would never want to be guilty of praying counter to the will of God, that is witchcraft, and it is blasphemous. It would be better for you and those in your bloodline to obey what God said, rather than to disobey God. If you don't know what God said, then pray in the Spirit or tarry in the presence of God until you know.

And, also stop making extra work for Jesus.

One Monkey

One monkey *don't* stop no show is considered to be an African American proverb. It is the title of a song that was first recorded in 1950. That was 75 years ago, but the phrase is still commonly used. For those who don't know, it means just because one person is not participating or cooperating in an effort or project, it doesn't mean that the work or progress will stop.

Saints of God, the Lord God's Plan will go forth, with or without you. It would be better for you, and those you know and love to obey God and get with God's Plan. It would be best for us all to stop making extra work for Jesus by cutting off the ears of people who shouldn't have their ears cut off and causing Jesus to have to stop what He is doing to heal that ear, (for example).

It would be better for us all to not cut off *people* from their God-given assignments if we are guilty of that.

Peter was loud, vociferous and aggressive, but the other, Judas had made that devil deal and was pretty quiet, sitting at dinner with Jesus. Judas didn't say much or anything from Bible accounts, while Peter, who was on Jesus' side but was kinda wild. Peter was wild and wrong, especially the night of Jesus' apprehension. We won't always know what *spirit* we are dealing with by how loud or how much they speak. God can roar like thunder, and He can also speak in a still small voice.

It is our responsibility to know the Voice of the Good Shepherd and not follow the voice of another.

We need to ask ourselves; how many things the Lord has to fix or work around because you didn't do what **He said**?

God said. That's what we do. If God had to do a work around, was it our fault? Was it your fault that you didn't obey? Was it rebellion, disobedience? Was it Ignorance? Did you not know how to do it? Or were you a blind follower without trying the *spirit*? Was it an issue of provision, you didn't have the help or the finances to do what God said? Else, why didn't you do it?

When God tells you to do a thing, often it is not until you start to do that thing that the Lord begins to help. God doesn't do for us what we should be doing ourselves.

Were you blindly following whomever or whatever you were following without *trying* the *spirit*?

If God said a thing, that always supersedes what a person--, male or female, or even a *monkey* or a donkey might say. You obey authority when you must. When God says that obedience is better than to sacrifice, He means obedience to God. Seek the Lord all day, every day.

Where was Peter and those Disciples after Jesus was apprehended what did they do? They went and hid. Did God tell them to go hide?

The women were at the Cross, after Jesus' death, but where were the men? Were they afraid of being apprehended or crucified themselves? If so, why were the women there? According to the historian, Josephus, women were subject to crucifixion as well as men. Why were the women there but not the men? Where were Jesus' Disciples? How much spiritual progress did they lose by hiding?

74

It seems the Disciples put themselves in *Time Out*. Did God say do that? Had they been misbehaving, to deserve Time Out? Well according to the Pharisees they were, so shutting down ministry, even for a moment or an hour, or ever how long they were in hiding was obeying man more than, or rather than obeying God.

Did the men stop doing ministry because the thing with Jesus didn't turn out as they expected it to? Did they sit themselves down? Did fear sit them down? What happened to the superseding Word of God? What happened to the Words that Jesus spoke as He activated them for ministry? Jesus didn't say that when He goes that ministry should stop. What sat them down? And, for how long? And what momentum did they lose in hiding instead of continuing to do ministry?

During that time period, who sat the Disciples down?

The Pharisees and the Romans who put fear in their hearts by what they saw Jesus go through. The Pharisees, the Sanhedrin, the High Priest all had something to do with sitting the Disciples down.

If the High Priest can do that, then you see what mere men, or men in authority, even church authority can do to other mere men. And, to women.

Then we recognize the damage done to ministry and ministers when they are shut down and sat down when God didn't say they should stop, pause, or cease ministry.

Yes, God can redeem the time and restore the years. God can restore you to right standing if He sat you down to purge you, prune you, chasten you, or teach you.

Too many have been sat down by humans when God said get up, stand up, stand, therefore--, then get up and obey God. God said--, but they did the opposite.

I Was Sat Down

While preaching one Sunday morning, I used the word, *stupid*. Well, it seems that *stupid* is a cuss word in the church I was attending. The founding father and mother of that church, who were my father-in-law and mother-in-law, appear to have gotten offended by that, and everything changed. I'm not Jesus but, in hindsight, the person I was married to, the founding father and mother's firstborn son and current "pastor" of the church was looking for a reason to sit me down, remove me, and divorce me. The word *stupid* seems to be what he or they were looking for.

No, I did not rail against any dignity. I did not call any person alive, or dead, in or out of the Bible, stupid. I was in the spirit and preaching about evangelism and I related how a frustrated, "pregnant" person might feel out in the field trying to witness while in the pangs of travail as outlined in Micah. Instead of using another adjective which could have really been offensive, since I don't talk like that, while in the heat of preaching, the word, stupid described the "field' that was uncomfortable, far from home, for a person in the travail of childbirth, far from normal conditions, and the use of this word set the local pharisees off.

Oh, what else did I do?

Yes, I did some other things in private, at home. I'd say it boiled down to two other things. One, I asked how a couple of gay guys who lived together could become deacons of that church? I asked the pastor, in private. Then I suggested to him, also in private, that because of their service if they should be promoted in their church roles, should they not be delivered first?

He laughed, uproariously.

And the final thing I did was to call not the pastor, but my husband out on a *seducing spirit* that he carried as he flirted with at least 70% of the women in the church. No, it was not my imagination.

A new music minister was hired. Just in passing, I was walking into the church with my husband on a choir rehearsal night. At that time, I learned that he greets the musician's wife, when she is not with her husband, by saying, *Hello, beautiful lady*, instead of by her name. She smiled politely. I said, "Hi Rhoda," calling her by her name. That music minister did not stay in the employ of that church very long. Wonder why.

One young couple who I had befriended were going through a medical issue. Well, it was the wife, not the husband who had the issue of blood, like the woman in the Bible. It was a spiritual issue, but I didn't realize it then, it was *eaters of flesh and drinkers of blood.* She had become very anemic and was homebound, even at her young age. But before that, she and I, along with two other women were chief friends. We talked all the time. We met for coffee every Monday, we had a jovial relationship. I was friends with other women in the church as well, but this particular group were the young ladies and more my age at that time.

My relationships with the older women were questioned by my husband who wanted to know why all my friends were older. He also wanted to know why didn't my younger friends ever come by the house?

I'm not sure if I knew it then, but it was really because he was there. That was not my reason, but I came to know that the women didn't want to come by there because he was there. I didn't really know why at that time.

Okay, so the younger woman with the issue of blood was homebound, anemic, and wasn't really eating anything but ice. We know that is a sign of iron deficiency, but there were at least three broken blenders in her house where she and her husband were constantly trying to crush ice for her.

I'd go to her house and cook for her family of four because she didn't feel like it, had no energy. I'd crush ice when one of their many blenders worked. I sat with her and kept her company for many days, and for hours and hours on those days.

Her husband would arrive home around 4:30 pm and he was a jokester and could make a dog laugh, actually. The problem with that was when he'd get home, he would make a big deal over me. There's his wife sitting there--, *what*? He'd make a big deal over me, come up to hug me and talk to me as if I was the only person in the room.

I hated it.

So, eventually, I'd go to their house and help her out, and sit with her, but would be sure to leave well before he returned home. His attention toward me was weird in my estimation, plus if his behavior would anger his wife, how was that going to lead to her becoming healed of what was diagnosed as a medical condition?

All that backstory was to let you all know that after divorcing the *pharisee* pastor, my anemic friend admitted to me that she had slept with him. She gave me the details of how it went down. I was surprised, but I was not surprised. She had obviously confessed to her husband, and all the attention *he* was giving me was her payback.

Who else did my pharisee pastor sleep with? Lots of them, probably; it was not my imagination. When I was sat down, which means demoted, from the pulpit to the front row that was because I sent two modesty scarves to a pretty lady and her pretty daughter who both sat on the front row in dresses, with their legs, how shall I say this?--, not closed. I am not kidding here. Thinking they were not aware of what they were doing, after all, the well-built child was 15 years old and her mother was doing it, so who could teach her? The other ladies in the church had noticed it too and were offended. So, it was left to me to handle this matter.

In a Sunday service, I discreetly sent a female usher with a modesty cloth for each of them. They waved off the usher and refused to cover up. When my pharisee husband, who obviously liked the sight of what they were showing him found out that I had sent modesty cloths to them he was furious.

One Sunday the congregants were asked to bring their offerings to the front and place them in the basket on the steps of the pulpit. This was different, usually the ushers passed the offering baskets. The congregants walked to the altar in what seemed like a decent and orderly fashion. However, I was standing there with my then-husband, and he spoke to exactly one person, in a soft, sweet, gushy, *Hi Susan* (not her real name.) And she smiled and said, *Hi* to him. He spoke to no one else who marched to the altar at that service. That was the front row lady who sat with skirt hiked and legs apart. I didn't ask him anything about this, but I gave him "the look" at the same time he looked at me to see if I heard or saw this exchange. Man, did he look guilty.

Next was my fall from the pulpit beside my husband, back to the front row.

As an afterthought, what if I was the one to choose one man in that congregation and speak to him sweetly as he came up to place his offering envelope in the basket? Uh huh--, you get my drift.

Yeah, let's move this First Lady/wife who has eyes to see and ears to hear out of the pulpit because it was messing up his mac or game, or whatever he was doing up there. By that time, I was named co-Pastor, not just First Lady.

Oh, I almost forgot, a video production team came to shoot a service to put together a new opening for the TV broadcast. Somehow in the final edits, the pretty lady who sat on the front row with her legs open was in a 1-minute opening twice and the pastor's wife was in the opening zero times. Pharisee-pastor is a micro-manager, the production crew did not do the final edits without his approval.

It was found out later that every service, for months, this woman was at church with another woman's husband, and she was also not divorced from whomever her husband was. But there she was sitting on the front row immodestly and adored by a pastor who had been married to his new wife for less than two years. This all came to a head one night during a prophetic conference when the wife of the man that *Susan* came to church with also came to church in the middle of the service, with his two children, making quite an entrance.

What happened next?

Nothing.

The cheating married man was promoted to Elder, and the immodest woman and he began to live together. But, I was long gone by then.

My point is, I was sat down for bogus reasons, seemingly because a man, even though he was the senior pastor of that church wanted to sin. God said to me, but then a man said differently.

Consider all of this when you look back on your own life if you were ever sat down, or shut up.

To this day, I use the word *stupid* as the Lord wills. I think my being sat down so a man could go into his flesh and entertain the people who were in their flesh was stupid. You've heard worse words than stupid from a pulpit, but what other people are saying, teaching, preaching, spewing out is not my guide. The Holy Spirit guides what words I can use in and out of the pulpit. But if the word, *stupid* was enough to get me out of that pharisee church, unholy marriage, and fake friendships, I am thankful.

In the process of all of that I was taken out of the pulpit and told to sit on the front row again. Later I was told that I'd be able to sit on the back row of the church only. This church wasn't even full, so there were rows of empty pews before you got to the back row.

I was exiled. Banned, placed outside of the gate. Was this supposed to be *outer darkness*?

We argued all week, most weeks. Well, he mostly argued; I usually just listened and prayed while he went on and on. Then one week he told me from then on, that I was now to sit on the back row of the church.

Why?

He had no real reason. It was more of a because I said so, and I'm in charge kinda thing. It was months before I found out that the word stupid was allegedly the cause of this. As if I could take it back? My message wasn't televised anyway, so what was the problem?

Wives, obey your husbands. But I refused to sit outside the gate, and I certainly was not going to be banished into outer darkness. So, the following week, for the first service in years, I refused to go to church with him; I stayed home. I'm telling you, after listening to him rant and **rage** all week, I could not stand the sound of that man's voice. Not today. Maybe another day, but not today.

Why didn't I "obey" my husband? Well folks, after *trying* the *spirit* that had tried to sit me down and banish me, I realized it was not my husband. Nor was that voice of God. It was *rage and whatever else traveled with rage*, which I learned that he hosted when it suited him. Therefore, I refused to obey that evil *spirit*.

Before he got home from church people were stopping by the house to check on me because he told the congregation that I wasn't in service because of illness. Folks, I was not sick. Well, to make matters worse, when he got home, I told him to never say to anyone that I am sick when I am not sick. I urged him by saying, "Do not tell lies on me." He hated that I said that all the more.

Once the demons in him said out loud to me, *"It's a shame a man can't control his wife these days."* The intention, I believe, was by using violence, since he threw a large box of business envelopes at me.

I ducked.

The rage in him tried to intimidate me one day, but I told it, *I am not afraid of you.*

I did come to learn that his family was afraid of that demon and whatever other demons he either entertained or whatever demons had captured his soul. Yet they didn't believe in deliverance. But as for his family, when the *spirit of rage* raged, they bowed, and he got his way in his family of birth.

Oh no. I'm not the one, and it is never the day, in the Name of Jesus. That didn't work on me. Saints of God, I have a brother who is not only like that, but worse than that. Ironically, the two of them have the same middle name. You can't make this stuff up.

So, he decided to sit me down at church. Why would a man want to humiliate his wife, especially when **he** is the active sinner? *Rage* and other demons were running this, not a man.

Try* every *spirit.

No man or woman has a heaven or hell to put you in; they also cannot banish you to outer darkness, especially if you have not blatantly sinned against their legalism, lies, and pharisaical structure.

God never said to me that I was doing too much in a church to require holiness, or at least decency. Sitting immodestly in a short skirt with your legs open in a church service is okay?, but don't say the word, *stupid*. Huh?

For a while I obeyed the church and marriage authority of that man, but then it got to be too much. He got his way, eventually I left after he filed for divorce. I would not file because God hates broken covenant, and I was not going to be the one to iniate the breaking of covenant.

Folks, I had to have a police presence to pack and move. They allowed me one day. Later I realized that the local authorities really know this man. I also later found out that many times his first wife had called the cops on him for what they labeled as domestic reasons. It was *rage*.

People, women, men—, all Christians, I urge you to pray, but also do your due diligence, do your research before marrying anyone. God can deliver any of us from anything and everything. But if we don't want to be delivered, if we want the demons such as *rage, lust, immodesty*, and *whoredoms*, they will simply remain.

I ask the Lord's forgiveness if I was **stupid** to stay in that "marriage" as long as I did. In my mind, I thought my marriage to a pastor would be a strong witness for my family and that they would be drawn to Christ by this. That's the main reason I stayed as long as I did.

(There is so much more to this story, but this is not even what I had planned to talk about in this book.)

Where Did I Go from There?

From there, saints of God you may not believe where I went. I went into hiding. I wasn't Elijah and I hadn't done any miracles on Mount Carmel, but I went into hiding. I wasn't David or anointed as king, but I went into hiding as if Saul was chasing me. Jesus was no longer on the Cross, and I wasn't a male Disciple, but I went into hiding. Yes, God told me to. Wisdom told me to.

The pharisee-pastor had become oddly dangerous and based on accounts of what I at that time began to hear that he did to his first wife, the one before me, I deemed him to be dangerous. (Why didn't someone tell me all this <u>before</u> I married him?)

Before I had eventually moved out, he threw me out of our matrimonial bedroom into the identical bedroom across the hall. Yes, I came home one day, and all of my things were moved into the guest bedroom across the hall. I stayed there a while, but then felt that the windows in that room were too large and too low to the ground, so I did not feel safe. One day when he wasn't home, I moved my belongings upstairs to a bedroom up there. Actually, I moved my things to two bedrooms upstairs, so he didn't know which one I was in at any given time.

I'm telling you, it was not safe there. I had called a locksmith and put a deadbolt lock on each of the doors with plans to wait it out until the divorce was final. My attorney had advised me not to move out of the house, although I wanted to. All my relatives were at least 800 miles away. He'd come home from wherever he went on any given day raging, about anything or nothing. Mostly I stayed in one of my rooms until he was gone, so we didn't bump into one another.

I had stopped going to the pharisee church and was visiting other churches, not to talk about this, but I visited other churches to continue congregational worship. Friends took me to churches they knew about.

I had no money. What I had was used to pay the retainer for a divorce lawyer that came highly recommended. But soon that lawyer hated me and was seemingly on the side of my then-husband. I believe he got to that lawyer and paid him off and he is a convincing liar.

I had no money because my then-husband said that no wife of his would work outside the home. So, I worked for the church for a small stipend, yet my living expenses were paid while in the parsonage. At the onset of his final tantrum against me, Rev. Pharisee stopped paying me. Period. And I had now moved and had overhead.

Control. Control is witchcraft.

Soon, churches in outlying areas started asking me to speak and preach on Sundays and I received some offerings. By this time, pastor Pharisee had split the church completely—I didn't split the church, and I never went to the new church that was formed by people he knew and had grown up with. Those who left, happened to be the moneymen of the pharisee church. They took at least half the members that were left from the half that was left when he divorced his first wife.

I did that for some months, waiting to sign final decree documents. Eventually the Lord gave me a word, *Why sit we here til' we die?* I packed up and came back to my home state and my own family.

And there were four leprous men at the entering in of the gate: and they said one to another, Why sit we here until we die? (2 Kings 7:3)

Was my family shocked? Oh yeah. Before we married, this man had written a letter to my parents asking for my hand in marriage and had wooed the entire family so they would love him. Else, I wouldn't have left my life and career and moved states away from home. What he didn't realize is that the way he treated me was far more important than anything that he could have promised that he would do.

Time went on and I had to waste time and money to fly back out to sign the final decree, but at least it was done.

So, this is the man I had married. This is the man that I gave authority over me in marriage and in my spiritual life in that church. Hindsight is 20/20. I should have seen better and chosen better, but in all things, we give thanks to the Lord for bringing us through.

Put It on Trial

Folks, if I had stayed sat down when I was sat down, you would have no messages, words, deliverance, prayers, or books from me. God said get up and he never said for me to sit down. What about you, if you've been sat down? What ministry is missing, what teaching or words of Wisdom? What about your books, videos, of podcasts that you should have made already? Are you a worship leader or a genuine intercessor? I started and did the warfare prayer in church before services; he sat that down. He tried to put other people in that position, but that's between him and God.

So, what happened to the person who sat me down?

What happened to anyone who has ever interfered with the Word of God or the ministry of God? What happens to anyone who interferes with the anointing that God has put on a person for God's own purposes?

Let's see: Jonah ended up in a whale. Spit out on a shore, scorched in the hot sun.

God says touch not his anointed, do His prophet no harm. **You** are God's anointed, if you are saved, you are anointed of God, where you go, who you see, who you minister to, who you witness to, give a cup of water to, who you bless, it is because God said, do the work of an evangelist.

You are a prophet; your words should build people up and tear down evil works. Sometimes you prophesy to yourself, but you are a prophet. David encouraged himself, in the Lord.

Saul despised the anointing on David: Saul ended up dead. Jezebel despised the anointing on Elijah; it didn't end up well for Jezebel at the hand of Jehu.

Anyone who tells you to shut up or be quiet when God tells you to speak and be a witness – well, you'd better *try* that *spirit* and obey God.

Now the Word says that we are to try every *spirit* . We try them by the Word of God, and we try them by the Fruit of the Spirit to see if they are of God or not.

But God is deep; you **try** people in Court. If this *spirit* is interfering and blocking what God said for you to do, then take them to the Courts of Heaven and report it to Heaven. Let the Lord know what's going on regarding you.

Sometimes what God says and what God said is in the Word of God. We are responsible to know what the Word says, it is why we read and study it. Man does not live by bread alone, but by every Word that proceeds out of God's mouth. When God is speaking, what He is saying is a *proceeding*, active, right now Word. It is our responsibility to hear that Word, receive that Word, and do that Word. It is our responsibility to know who or what said it and what *spirit* was behind the mouth that spoke it. When it is God, then we obey. Amen.

God is First

God said..., but then a man said: God is always first because He is God, but He is first because in the Beginning was the Word and the Word was God. God was first and we were formed and made and breathed life into afterward. God first. God first loved us. God is first, always.

As you *try* the *spirit* that is speaking through that man, ask God, Father, does this match the timeline you have for my life? Do I obey this? Do I proceed or do I stop here and rest? Do I stop here to listen? Do I stop here to learn? Do I apologize here and then quickly repent? Or, Father, should I be standing, moving, walking, running my race right now? Should I be mounting up with wings like an eagle? Or do I sit here? Do I, like Joseph, take a punishment for something I did not do?

Is this a test of forgiving 70 times 7? Yes, I forgive. I forgave a lot and attempted to move on. Saints of God, I apologized to that pharisee pastor oppressively. I apologized to him almost every day of the week because he was constantly offended by me or something I did or would say. I did it to make the peace—, agreeing with my adversary quickly. (A spouse should never be your adversary.)

An apology is not what he wanted; it was never what he wanted. He wanted to fight. I refused to fight him. Instead, I spoke the Word and that angered him even more.

That foolishness stopped the day I apologized again for something I didn't do but he said I didn't apologize right. So, he had me apologize to him for this alleged infraction 13 times. **Thirteen times** on the same day, in the same conversation, in succession. Thirteen times. No, try as he may, he was not able to break my spirit. It took me a while but that is the day and the moment that I realized that this man is abusive; this is impossible, and I'm not doing it anymore.

Yup, I tried that *spirit--*, those *spirits*, and I was done.

For instance? This man would be angry with me because he'd have me stand up and introduce him, as if no one knew who he was--, he'd been pastoring for at least a dozen years by then. But he'd be angry because he said that other pastor's wives said all kinds of nice things about them, but I never said anything good about him.

What?

So, I tuned in to what some of these wives said when they introduced their pastor-spouse. One introduction he especially liked was when a young wife told the congregation that her husband had saved her life. This man didn't save my life, so how could I say that? Then I realized that I couldn't say anything nice about him because there was nothing nice to say. It was nice of me not to say anything bad about him, especially given what I'm writing about in this book. I spent most of the marriage thinking it was wise to *cover* your husband. I didn't want to spill all of this and hurt the church. Saints, it was never my intention to write about this, but not only here it is, but there is so much more.

In addition, some of those pastors had been married to their wives 15 and 20+ years, had children together and had built a life together. My pharisee pastor and I had been married a couple of years by then. Now began my fervent prayer for the Lord to help him grow up and for whatever had arrested his development might itself be arrested and let him grow up. (That's another whole story.)

Will You Just Sit There?

The lepers sat outside the Gate. Mostly that is what people do outside the gate--, they sit. If you 've been sat down, that is the usual intention.

And there were four leprous men at the entering in of the gate: and they said one to another, Why sit we here until we die? (2 Kings 7:3)

In business it is called *constructive firing*. If your hours are reduced to four hours a week, for example, the employer is waiting for you to quit without firing you. You will "fire" yourself, and leave. Do you leave, or do you fight that? God will have to answer it for you. People do this in interpersonal relationships as well--, they mistreat the other person or even *ghost* them so the other person will leave them and they don't have to break up with the person. It's weak and cowardly, but people do it.

People do it in households where they mistreat a person so badly that they will move out. All of that is manipulation and domination and it is witchcraft. So, who wants to live with or work with a witch anyway? Only another witch, but there is no guarantee that they will even get along.

Whatever you ask God, He will tell you, Yes or No.

Now if you get shut down and sat down, ask the Lord: *Does this match the timeline for my destiny?* Should I be parked on this pew? God will tell you, Yes or No.

This book is not about fighting with or arguing with anyone – it is about what God said to **you** about what you should be doing in the Earth.

And this is not a bondage message. But don't let it be a *can't-get-there-from-here* issue for you. You know if you don't do certain updates on your computer then the next patch or fix comes along, it won't *take*, and it ends up that you can't get there from where you are because you missed too many updates. If you are sitting down when you should be standing up, you could miss spiritual updates. How much progress are you losing when you are not doing what you are supposed to be doing either because you are out of place out of condition, or you've been defiled? If someone has made you sit down when you should not be sitting down, this may be the start of you getting in a lot of trouble with God.

As said before, this is not a bondage message. I'm not telling you that if you don't go to the next prayer meeting you are really going to miss out.

Miss out on what?

I don't know, but yes, I want to be there if that particular seminar, conference or meeting is pivotal for my spiritual development, because I don't want a *can't get there from here* problem in the future by missing out on the updates.

I do not care if I miss out on entertainment. But unless the Lord God sat us down, we are missing out every time we are sat down by a man who is countering the Word that God gave you.

Some feel they can't miss one thing, and they spend far too much time trying to do everything, support everything, pray in every watch by sleeping 2 hours out of every three to be sure to pray one hour in every watch. How is this humanly possible? But I think I know someone who tries to do that; they have no job.

Sometimes the Lord is teaching you obedience, followship, or patience. It is peculiar between you and the Lord. So you have to talk to Him all the time to know if you are progressing or regressing, stagnant, disobedient, or wasting time.

But if you get shut down or sat down and stay down because you are having a pout fest or giving up, because *that will show them, won't it*? That is not God. I don't care what they said to you or how they hurt your feelings. Your feelings are not supposed to be running your life. It doesn't matter what *they* said; if it was not of God, it certainly could have been very cruel. It could have been nice-nasty--, some people have that kind of venom in their words.

But God can restore your soul, so what? So, forgive them, and move on. You can be healed from a broken heart or hurt feelings.

Beloved, be in health and prosper even as your soul prospers.(3 John 2)

Ask the Lord to restore your soul, heal you emotionally, make you emotionally strong, and get up and do the work that the Lord has assigned you to do, in the Name of Jesus. **Amen.**

Prayers

1. Lord, have Mercy on me, a sinner. If I am none of Yours give me a Godly sorrow for my sins and make me one of Yours. Lord, come into my heart today and be the Lord of my life, in the Name of Jesus, Amen.

2. Father, fill me with Your Holy Spirit that I may hear from Heaven and that my prayer life will be assisted, in the Name of Jesus.

3. Lord, I repent of all disobedience, rebellion, and procrastination, idolatry, complacency, laziness, moodiness, in the Name of Jesus.

4. Let the Love that You gave Jesus for us be in me as I love others that You have sent me to minister to in my unique administration of the Gifts of the Spirit.

5. Lord, forgive me for not loving Your people, in the Name of Jesus.

6. Father, forgive me for not forgiving; I endeavor from now on to be a very understanding and forgiving person, in the Name of Jesus.

7. Father, I dislodge, loose, and remove all *jealousy* from the gates of my life, in the Name of Jesus.

8. Forgive me for not ministering to Your people when You have said to do it, in the Name of Jesus.

9. Father, if I am outside the gate for any reason, lift up ye heads o ye gates! I am with the King of Glory and by Your Mercy Lord, let me back into fellowship and into right standing with **You** and Your people, in the Name of Jesus.

10. Father, redeem the time, restore the years, in the Name of Jesus.

11. Lord, reset my destiny clock; put me back on Your time, in the Name of Jesus.

12. Father, reset my destiny calendar to where I should be right now, in Kingdom time, in the Name of Jesus.

13. Burn up, destroy and dismantle any evil, witchcraft, demonic or occultic timelines, calendars, or clocks that are programmed against my life, in the Name of Jesus.

14. Father, if my vehicle of destiny is up on blocks for any reason, please help me get it repaired, restored, renewed, and powered up to take me everywhere I need to go for destiny and to the Praise of Your Glory. Amen.

15. Lord, by Holy Ghost Fire, I burn every evil track that takes me into an evil timeline, in the Name of Jesus.

16. I declare and decree that I will stay on track and on time for destiny, in the Name of Jesus.

17. By Thunder Fire of God, I blast every obstacle, barrier, and blockage out of my way, in the Name of Jesus.

18. Father, let my children see me reach destiny so they too will be inspired and fired up to do the same, all to the Praise of Your Glory, Amen.

19. Father, Your Voice, let me hear Your Voice every day and in everything, and do not let me follow the voice of another, a stranger, a liar, or a thief, either knowingly or unknowingly, in the Name of Jesus.

20. God said it, that's enough for me, in the Name of Jesus.

21. Lord, silence the voices of flesh, of *error*, the naysayers, the unsaved, and all demonic, witchcraft, or occultic voices in my life, in the Name of Jesus.

22. I declare **PEACE**. Peace be still, so I can hear even the still small voice of the Lord, if that is how He chooses to speak, in the Name of Jesus.

23. Father, I possess all things that pertain to my Peace, and peace is my umpire as I do the will of the One who sent me, the Only Living God, Amen.

24. Lord, in the Name of Jesus, I ask that You make me fruitful with Fruit that remains and that I do not waste time.

25. And Lord, do not let time waste me, in the Name of Jesus. Amen

Psalm 29

Give unto the Lord, O ye mighty, give
unto the Lord glory and strength.

Give unto the Lord the glory due unto his
name; worship the Lord in the beauty of
holiness.

The voice of the Lord is upon the waters:
the God of glory thundereth: the Lord is
upon many waters.

The voice of the Lord is powerful; the
voice of the Lord is full of majesty.

The voice of the Lord breaketh the cedars;
yea, the Lord breaketh the cedars of
Lebanon.

He maketh them also to skip like a calf;
Lebanon and Sirion like a young unicorn.

The voice of the Lord divideth the flames
of fire.

The voice of the Lord shaketh the
wilderness; the Lord shaketh the
wilderness of Kadesh.

The voice of the Lord maketh the hinds to calve, and discovereth the forests: and in his temple doth every one speak of his glory.

The Lord sitteth upon the flood; yea, the Lord sitteth King for ever. Amen.

You Can't Shut God's Mouth

God said it, and that's enough for me. When God opens His mouth and says something, then a man counters what God said that is the same as that man shutting the mouth of God.

Is that man serious, right now? In anger, rage or jealousy, has he thought this all the way through?

No, God's mouth through which His proceeding words and decrees flow are a door that cannot be shut. No man can shut it. Amen.

Hearing God's voice and obeying is a strong sign of having a teachable spirit. You can tell some people things, but they don't listen or heed. The rebellious child or rambunctious teen seems to have to go through things for themselves before they learn. And that *going through* is usually tough. I usually say, *Hey, you can just <u>tell</u> me something and I'll believe you.* Fire burns if you touch it. Ice is cold –, you can just tell me. I don't need to stick my hand into a fire. But there are doubting Thomases, there are people from Missouri who need you to show them before they believe something.

God said something? That's good enough. Unless I don't understand, I will just do or at least try to do what He said. If God tells you something, that you don't comprehend, ask Him again. Ask Him to show you again. Ask Him what does that mean or how do I do that? Ask for more details. And if other people are involved in facilitating what the Lord said, ask for those people, because sometimes we may only have part of the vision.

Don't just slough off something God told you to do because you don't understand it. Don't ignore God, grieving and quenching the Holy Spirit. Don't change what God said because you don't like what He said. Don't change what God said because you don't like the people, He assigned you to. Don't change what God said for you to do because a man said otherwise, unless you know that is a superseding command from God spoken by a person of God. Don't let a sly or seasoned lying voice slither into your life like the Serpent and change what you know God told you to do.

Do not let your friends talk you out of it or let your enemies steer you away from obeying God. Do not let lust and winds of doctrine draw you away from your destiny.

If You Have Authority

To the person who knows he has the authority to shut others down, shut them up, or sit them down, be very wise. Be very careful. Be very discerning that you know that you know that you are hearing from God. Whether you are in a business setting or in a church, do not abuse God-given authority.

Parents, be very careful that you don't shut your kid down. So, your child wants to be a brain surgeon? Let them pursue that goal and that dream until it is discovered that they really don't want to do that. Do not shut another person down from pursuing their own dreams and definitely don't malign and depress them so much that they don't do anything at all.

Who knows, the brain surgeon student may end up being an internist and find love for medicine and healing there. They could end up being a florist, but each person should be entitled to follow their dream, their heart, or whatever God has put in their spirit to do and become.

Never be so power struck that you belittle or hurt others in order to make yourself feel big. Never hurt others just because you can.

God will strongly judge abuse of power and those who oppress others. God judges those in authority differently. For example, teachers will be judged differently. Jezebel called herself a *teacher*. Lying to and sitting people down is oppression; God strongly judges those who oppress the poor, and children.

Prophets who can be bought for money or fame will be judged strongly if they lead people astray. Even if you get powers or evil anointing from the dark kingdom and never repent, God will judge that; especially if you get the powers or anointing to do succeed in life while doing harm to others and not caring.

He is the Righteous Judge; He can and will judge us all.

26. I seal these words, prayers, decrees, declarations across every dimension, realm, era, timeline, past, present and future to infinity. I seal them with the Blood of Jesus and the Holy Spirit of Promise.

27. Every retaliation against these words, prayers, decrees, declarations against the speaker, the reader, or anyone who prays these prayers at any time in the future, backfire with reverb against the evil perpetrator to infinity, without Mercy, in the Name of Jesus Christ.

Amen.

Then shall I not be ashamed, when I have **respect** unto all thy commandments. (Psalm 119:6)

Dear Reader

If God told you or if a true representative of God told you to sit down, then sit down. Else, stand up, stand boldly, stand therefore and do the work that the Lord has assigned you to do. Now where you do it should not be a point of contention. Let the Lord lead you to the place and places where you learn, grow, and share.

So, stay prayerful and faithful; the Lord will deliver. Amen.

Shalom,

Dr. Marlene Miles

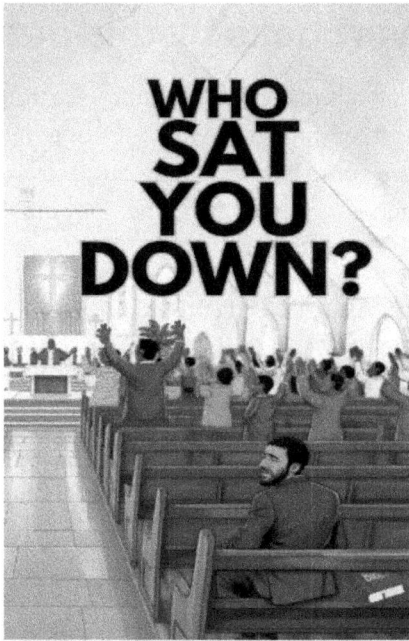

Thank you for acquiring and reading this book and supporting this ministry. This book is based on the message: God Said… then a man said…
https://studio.youtube.com/video/x3QJfJb9xmY/edit

There are many more messages the Dr. Marlene Miles You Tube Channel

Prayerbooks by this author

While most books by this author have prayer points either throughout the book or at the end, there are some books that are only prayers. You just open up the book and pray. They are listed below:

Prayers Against Barrenness: *For Success in Business and Life*

Fruit of the Womb: *Prayers Against Barrenness*

Beauty Curses, *Warfare Prayers Against*
https://a.co/d/5Xlc20M

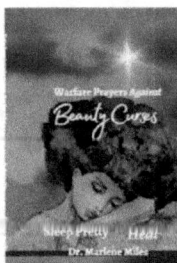

Courts of Marriage: Prayers for Marriage in the Courts of Heaven
(prayerbook) https://a.co/d/cNAdgAq

Courtroom Warfare @ Midnight
(prayerbook) https://a.co/d/5fc7Qdp

Demonic Cobwebs *(prayerbook)*
https://a.co/d/fp9Oa2H

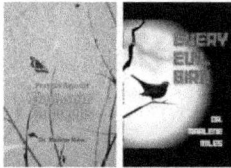

Every Evil Bird https://a.co/d/hF1kh1O

Gates of Thanksgiving

Spirits of Death, Hell & the Grave, Pass Over Me and My House

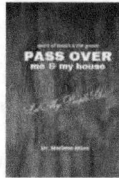

Throne of Grace: Courtroom Prayer

Warfare Prayer Against Poverty
https://a.co/d/bZ611Yu

Other books by this author

AK: The Adventures of the Agape Kid

Already Married in the Spirit: *Why You May Not Be Married in the Natural*

AMONG SOME THIEVES

Ancestral Powers

Anti-Marriage, *The Spirit of*

Backstabbers https://a.co/d/gi8iBxf

Barrenness, *Prayers Against* https://a.co/d/feUltIs

Battlefield of Marriage, *The*

Beware of the Dog: Prayers Against Dogs in the Dream.

Bless Your Food: *Let the Dining Table be Undefiled*

Blindsided: *Has the Old Man Bewitched You?* https://a.co/d/5O2fLLR

Break Free from Collective Captivity

Broken Spirits & Dry Bones

By Means of a Whorish Father: What Happens to the Children?
https://a.co/d/cV3fT4D

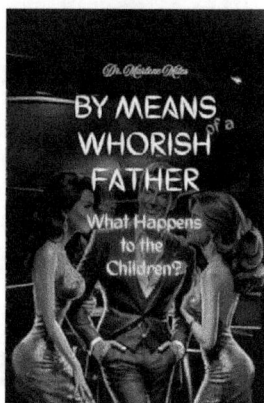

Casting Down Imaginations

Churchzilla, The Wanna-Be, Supposed-to-be Bride of Christ

Demonic Cobwebs (prayerbook)

Demonic Time Bombs

Demons Hate Questions

Devil Loves Trauma, *The*

Devil Weapons: Unforgiveness, Bitterness,…

The Devourers: Thieves of Darkness 2

Do Not Swear by the Moon

Don't Refuse Me, Lord (4 book series)

https://a.co/d/idP34LG

Dream Defilement

The Emptiers: *Thieves of Darkness, 1*
https://a.co/d/5I4n5mc

Evil Touch

Failed Assignment

Fantasy Spirit Spouse
https://a.co/d/hW7oYbX

FAT Demons (The): *Breaking Demonic Curses* https://a.co/d/4kP8wV1

The Fold (5-book series)

- The Fold (Book 1)
- Name Your Seed (Book 2)
- The Poor Attitudes of Money (3)
- Do Not Orphan Your Seed (4)
- For the Sake of the Gospel (5)
- My Sowing Journal

Gang Ups: Touch Not God's Anointed

Getting Rid of Evil Spiritual Food

https://a.co/d/i2L3WYQ

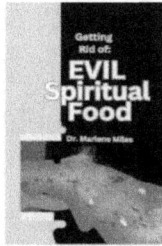

got HEALING? Verses for Life

got LOVE? Verses for Life

got HOPE? Verses for Life

got money? https://a.co/d/g2av41N

Here Come the Horns: *Skilled to Destroy*
https://a.co/d/cZiNnkP

Hidden Sins: Hidden Iniquity

https://a.co/d/4Mth0wa

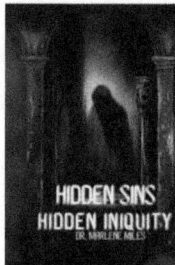

How to Dental Assist

How to Dental Assist2: Be Productive, Not Wasteful

How to STOP Being a Blind Witch or Warlock

I Take It Back

Legacy

Let Me Have A Dollar's Worth
https://a.co/d/h8F8XgE

Level the Playing Field

Living for the NOW of God

Lose My Location
https://a.co/d/crD6mV9

Love Breaks Your Heart

Made Perfect In Love

Man Safari, *The*

Marriage Ed. Rules of Engagement & Marriage

Made Perfect in Love

Money Hunters: Beware of Those

Money on the Altar https://a.co/d/4EqJ2Nr

Mulberry Tree, *The*
https://a.co/d/9nR9rRb

Motherboard (The) - *Soul Prosperity Series*

Name Your Seed

Occupy: *Until I Return*

Plantation Souls

Players Gonna Play

Power Money: Nine Times the Tithe

https://a.co/d/gRt41gy

The Power of Wealth *(forthcoming)*

Powers Above

The Robe, Part 1, The Lessons of Joseph

The Robe, Part II, The Lessons of Joseph

Seasons of Grief

Seasons of Waiting

Seasons of War

Second Marriage, Third--, *Any Marriage*

https://a.co/d/6m6GN4N

Seducing Spirits: Idolatry & Whoredoms

https://a.co/d/4Jq4WEs

Shut the Front Door: *Prayers to Close Portals*

Sift You Like Wheat

Six Men Short: What Has Happened to all the Men?

Soul Prosperity soul prosperity series 3

https://a.co/d/5p8YvCN

Souls Captivity soul prosperity series 2

The Spirit of Anti-Marriage

The Spirit of Poverty

StarStruck

SUNBLOCK

The Swallowers: *Thieves of Darkness*, 3

Take It Back

This Is NOT That: How to Keep Demons from Coming at You

Time Is of the Essence

Too Many Wives: *Why You Have Lady Problems*

Tormenting Spirits
https://a.co/d/dAogEJf

Toxic Souls

Triangular Power *(series)*

- Powers Above
- SUNBLOCK
- Do Not Swear by the Moon
- STARSTRUCK

Unbreak My Heart: *Don't Let Me Die*

Uncontested Doom

Unguarded Hours, *The*

Unseen Life, *The* (forthcoming)

Upgrade: How to Get Out of Survival Mode

- Toxic Souls (Book 2 of series)
- Legacy (Book 3 of series)

The Wasters: *Thieves of Darkness,* Bk 2
https://a.co/d/bUvI9Jo

What Have You to Declare? What Do You Have With You from Where You've Been?

When I Was A Child, *I Prayed As a Child*

When the Devourer is Rebuked

https://a.co/d/1HVv8oq

Who Sat You Down?

The Wilderness Romance *(series)* This series is about conducting a Godly relationship and marriage with someone who is a Wilderness person. It is about how to recognize it and navigate through it. These books are about how not to get caught up in such.

- *The Social Wilderness*
- *The Sexual Wilderness*
- *The Spiritual Wilderness*

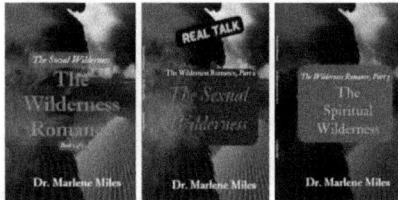

Other Series

The Fold (a series on Godly finances)
https://a.co/d/4hz3unj

Soul Prosperity Series
https://a.co/d/bz2M42q

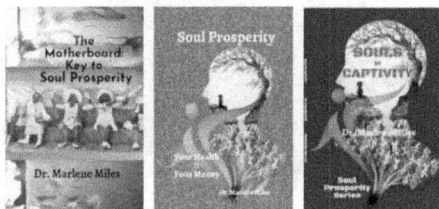

Spirit Spouse books

https://a.co/d/9VehDSo

https://a.co/d/97sKOwm

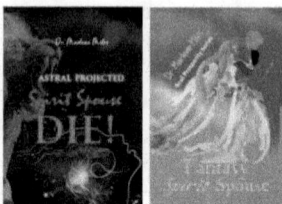

Battlefield of Marriage, The

https://a.co/d/eUDzizO

Players Gonna Play

https://a.co/d/2hzGw3N

Matters of the Heart

Made Perfect in Love
https://a.co/d/7OMQW3O

Love Breaks Your Heart
https://a.co/d/4KvuQLZ

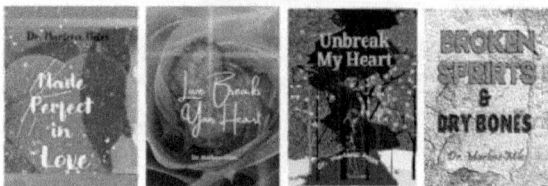

Unbreak My Heart
https://a.co/d/84ceZ6M

Broken Spirits & Dry Bones
https://a.co/d/e6iedNP

Thieves of Darkness series

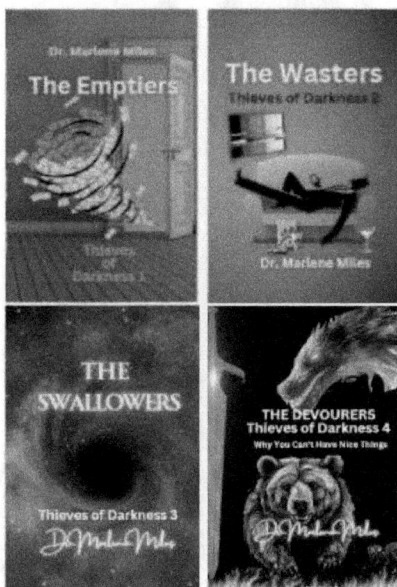

The Emptiers https://a.co/d/heio0dO

The Wasters https://a.co/d/5TG1iNQ

The Swallowers
https://a.co/d/1jWhM6G

The Devourers: Why We Can't Have Nice Things https://a.co/d/87Tejbf

Triangular Powers https://a.co/d/aUCjAWC

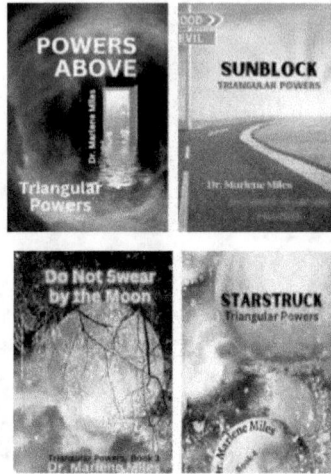

Upgrade (series) *How to Get Out of Survival Mode* https://a.co/d/aTERhX0